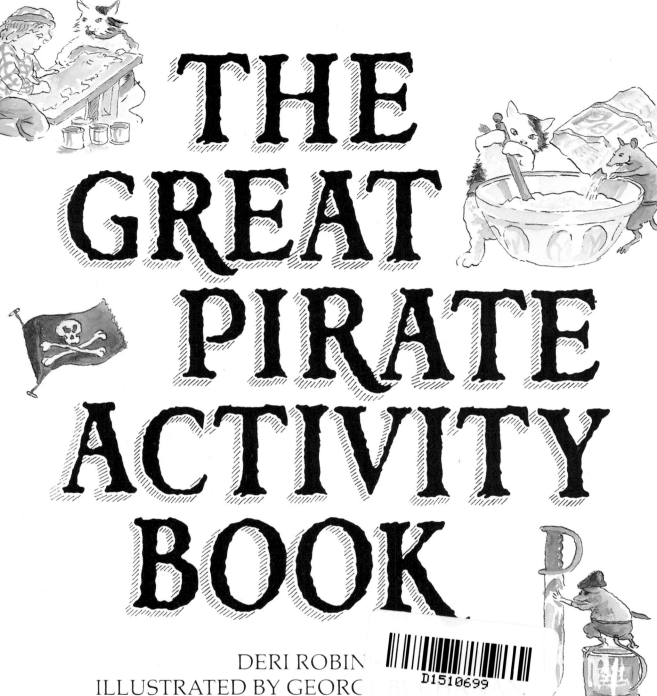

# THE GREAT PIRATE ACTIVITY BOOK

DERI ROBIN

ILLUSTRATED BY GEORG

**KINGFISHER**

NEW YORK

KINGFISHER
Larousse Kingfisher Chambers Inc.
95 Madison Avenue
New York, New York 10016

First edition 1995
4 6 8 10 9 7 5
4TR / 1098 / EDK / HBM(HBM) / 140ARG
Text copyright © Larousse plc 1994
Illustrations copyright © George Buchanan 1994

LIBRARY OF CONGRESS CATALOGING-IN-PUBLICATION DATA
Robins, Deri
The Great Pirate Activity Book/Deri Robins:
illustrated by George Buchanan.
p. cm.
1. Creative activities and seas work: Juvenile literature.
2. Pirates — Juvenile literature. [1. Pirates. 2. Handicraft.]
I. Buchanan. George. ill. II. title.
GV1203. R5719 1995
790. 1'922–dc20 94-43140 CIP AC

ISBN 1-85697-578-9
Printed in Spain
Designed by John Jamieson
Cover design by Terry Woodley

# CONTENTS

# SO, YOU WANT TO BE A PIRATE?

Have you ever longed to sail the seven seas in search of thrills and adventure? If so, why not become a pirate? In this book you can read about some of the wickedest pirates that ever lived. You can also find out how to make a hook, design a Jolly Roger, build a pirate ship, and turn your bedroom into a captain's cabin! All you need is a basic kit like the one shown below.

## WHAT YOU NEED

For most of the activities in this book, you'll need some cardboard, paper, paints, scissors, and glue. Some of the activities need special ingredients, such as flour, split peas, or a tea bag!

A COAT HANGER

OLD CEREAL BOXES

BRUSHES

SCISSORS

PENCILS

FELT-TIPPED PENS

STRING

POSTER PAINTS

## THE SPANISH MAIN

Pirates have roamed the seas since ancient times, and some are still around today. But perhaps the most famous of all are the ones who sailed along the Spanish Main about 300 years ago.

The Spanish Main was the name given to Central America, which Spain had invaded in the 1500s. Spanish soldiers stole gold and precious jewels that belonged to the Native Americans and loaded them onto huge galleons to take back home. The pirates then robbed the Spanish galleons!

## TREASURES FROM THE EAST

During the 1600s, the English often used pirates as a weapon in their war against Spain. Some pirates were even knighted for their efforts! However, once peace was made between the two countries, the laws against piracy were toughened. Many pirates headed for the Orient, where trading ships were returning to Europe laden with riches.

## PIRATES AND PRIVATEERS

Real pirates robbed any ship they wished and kept the booty for themselves. Privateers, on the other hand, worked for their government. They carried special documents that allowed them to plunder any ship that belonged to the enemy.

CARDBOARD AND PAPER

DOWEL

FLOUR

GLUE

OLD NEWSPAPERS

SCRAPS OF CLOTH AND OLD CLOTHES

TAPE

# A SHORT LIFE, BUT A MERRY ONE

Being a pirate wasn't always exciting. Sometimes whole months went by without anything happening at all!

In between raids, there were plenty of chores for the pirates to do. Musicians played jolly sea chanties to make the daily tasks go with a swing...

... and to help them while away the long, moonlit evenings at sea.

Pirates spent a lot of their free time playing cards and dice. They also liked to dance and sing, and to drink rum and brandy— when they could get it!

The food was revolting. Meat and fish had to be smothered in salt to stop them from spoiling. There were no fresh fruits or vegetables either, so the crew often came down with horrible illnesses such as scurvy.

Instead of bread, the pirates ate moldy biscuits called "hard tack." These were often crawling with weevils after a few weeks at sea.

With a bit of luck, a pirate might be able to survive the food. However, he could still catch all kinds of ghastly diseases from the rats and bugs that scurried all over the ship...

The company on board a pirate ship was usually rough and dangerous. Some of the crew were thieves or murderers who had escaped from prison. Others had been mutineers or had deserted from the army or the navy.

A pirate's life was full of risks and danger. If he wasn't killed during battle or poisoned by the food, he could easily end up in the hangman's noose! Although many captured pirates were pardoned, the ringleaders were usually hung for their crimes.

Many pirates had once been honest sailors but had become tired of the harsh discipline and cruel captains. In many ways, life on board a pirate ship was a vacation after the navy!

But the main reason that men (and a few women) became pirates was the thought of getting rich quickly. Pirates could make more money out of one lucky raid than an honest sailor could earn in all his years at sea!

So, if the life was so hard and dangerous, why did people become pirates?

A lot of men ran away to sea to escape an even more miserable life on land. Some were fed up with the lack of jobs back home. Others had run away from jail, slave owners, or unhappy marriages!

Even if they never managed to capture a treasure galleon, pirates could make a very good living from robbing small merchant ships of their cargo of cloth, spices, brandy, and tobacco, and selling it at the nearest port.

# THE COMPLETE PIRATE KIT

Most pirates wore loose, baggy clothing that allowed them to move easily around the ship. Whenever they captured any well-dressed prisoners, they'd take the best clothing for themselves!

## BASIC KIT

**1** All you need is an old pair of pants or jeans and a T-shirt—cut ragged edges with scissors and add patches if you like.

**2** Tie a scarf around your head— you could also sew a hoop earring or a curtain ring to the side. Or just tie the scarf around your neck.

**3** Tie a big scarf around your waist, and buckle on a belt (you'll need it to hold your cutlass in place).

Pirates were always losing bits of themselves in battle. Here's how to make an eyepatch and a hook...

For the eyepatch, you will need: some black paper, elastic, scissors, and some glue

For the hook, you will need: a plastic bottle, scissors, a plastic coat hanger, and some black latex paint

## EYEPATCH

**1** Cut a semicircle from black paper, and fold over one edge.

**2** Lay a piece of elastic along the crease, and glue down the edge. Tie the ends in a knot, making sure that it fits around your head comfortably.

## HOOK

CUT AN "X" HERE

SNAP OFF HOOK

**1** Cut the end off a plastic bottle. Cut an "X" in the bottom.

**2** Paint the bottle with black paint and leave it to dry.

**3** Ask an adult to snap the hook off a plastic coat hanger.

**4** Push the hook through the "X". Put your hand inside the bottle and hold the broken end of the hook.

# Captain's Kit

Many captains dressed in fine clothes—even during battle! Back in the 1600s, this meant a lot of ruffled shirts, fancy jackets and vests, and some very large hats...

## CAPTAIN'S CLOTHES

**1** Sew shiny buttons onto a jacket. Add lace for extra glamour.

**2** Tuck a pair of pants into a pair of galoshes.

## CAPTAIN'S HAT

*You will need:
black cardboard
(15 x 18 inches), scissors,
stapler, and white paper*

**1** Fold the cardboard in half and copy the pattern. Cut out both pieces and staple the sides together.

**2** Paint a skull and crossbones on one side of the hat using thick white poster paint.

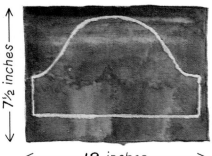

7½ inches

18 inches

CUT A FEATHER FROM
PAPER AND STAPLE
TO HAT

10

# PIRATE WEAPONS

To make these weapons, you will need: some cardboard, scissors, newspaper, wallpaper paste, poster paints, and some clear polyurethane varnish

DAGGER

CUTLASS

3 inches

6 inches

7 inches

15 inches

**1** Copy the cutlass and dagger onto cardboard. Cut them out with scissors.

**2** Mix the paste, following the directions given on the package.

**3** Tear several sheets of newspaper into small strips. Dip them into the paste and smooth them over the weapons until they're covered. Leave to dry.

**4** Repeat with two more layers. When dry, paint with silver and brown paint. Finish with a coat of varnish.

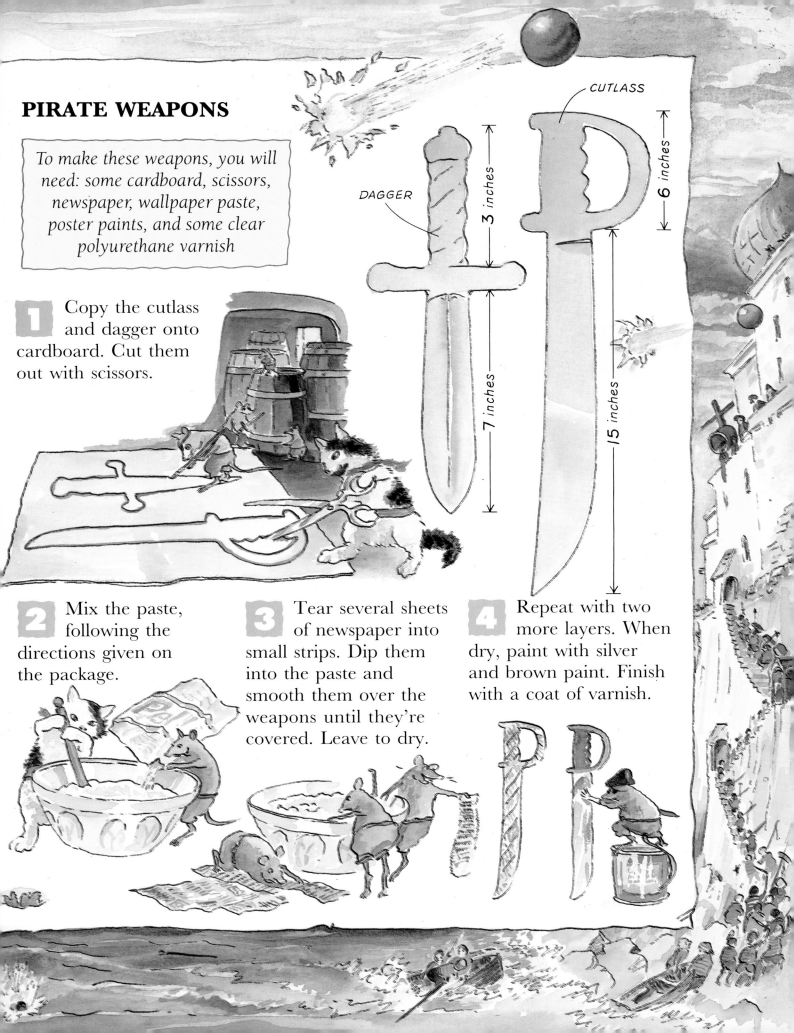

# FAIR SHARES AND ROUGH JUSTICE

Although pirates were ruthless thieves and murderers, they lived by a strict set of rules that they drew up themselves.

## THE CAPTAIN

The ship was owned by the crew, and the crew elected the captain.

They obeyed him in battle, but at other times he could be outvoted—or even removed from his position!

## THE RULES

All crew members had to sign a list of rules, called articles. If there wasn't a Bible handy, they swore on a hatchet to uphold them!

*All treasure, liquor, and other gains were shared equally among the crew— although the captain and his officers all got extra shares.*

*Any pirate caught striking a shipmate on board the ship would be flogged. All arguments had to be settled on land, when they reached port.*

## PIRATE PUNISHMENTS

Pirates were very hard on any shipmate who broke the rules.

Although walking the plank is a well-known punishment, it probably never happened!

Marooning was a fate worse than death. The pirate was left on a deserted island with only a gun, some shot, and some water.

For small crimes, a pirate might be flogged with the "cat o'nine tails"—a stick with nine pieces of knotted rope.

If a pirate was "keel-hauled," he was dangled overboard, pulled under the ship, and scraped against the rough barnacles underneath.

*Gambling for money was forbidden on board some ships.*

*For an eye or limb lost in battle, a pirate would receive an injury payment (for example, around $600 for a leg).*

*All weapons had to be kept clean and ready for service.*

*No women were allowed on board— though there were some exceptions to this rule!*

# CAPTAIN'S CABIN

Here's how to turn a corner of your own bedroom into a captain's cabin...

## PORTHOLE

*You will need: cardboard, a saucepan lid, some split peas, scissors, glue, and poster paints*

**1** Put the lid on the cardboard. Draw around it and cut out the shape.

**2** Draw another circle inside the first one, to make the rim. Then glue split peas around the rim, to make "rivets."

## TELESCOPE

*You will need: three squares of thick paper (about 8 inches wide), paper clips, scissors, glue, paints, and brushes*

**1** Roll up a piece of paper, and glue it down the side.

**2** Roll up another piece. Push it into the first tube and let go so that it fills the space.

PAPER CLIPS HOLD TUBE TOGETHER WHILE GLUE DRIES

## LOGBOOK

*You will need: a notebook with a stiff cover, cardboard, string, glue, paints, and brushes*

**1** Cut shapes from cardboard, and glue them on the book.

## ANCIENT MAP

*You will need: thick white paper, a ballpoint pen, and a damp, used tea bag*

**1** Draw a map with the ballpoint pen—you could trace a piece of coastline from an atlas, or invent your own.

**3** Paint the rim gold or silver.

**4** Paint a view in the middle!

"RIVETS"

**3** Pull it out and glue the sides.

**4** Make a third tube. Then push the tubes back inside each other.

PAINT THE TELESCOPE

**2** Coil pieces of string and glue them on, too.

**3** Brush gold paint all over the book and leave to dry. Then rub a little black paint along the edges of the cardboard and string.

**2** Press the tea bag all over the map. To make it look old, try folding it up and tearing the edges.

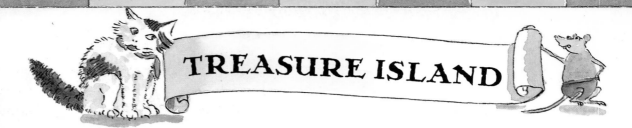

# TREASURE ISLAND

Here's a treasure-hunting game for two, three, or four pirates to play. You'll need a die, and a coin or a button for each player.

FOULED ANCHOR. GO BACK TO SHIP.

CHASED BY CROCODILES! MOVE TO 10

RUN FOR YOUR LIFE! MOVE TO 14

MARCH ALL THROUGH THE NIGHT. TAKE ANOTHER TURN.

FORGOT GROG AND VICTUALS. GO BACK TO SHIP.

ROPE LADDER LOOKS UNSAFE. MISS A TURN WHILE YOU FIX IT.

SLIP ON STEPPING STONES. SWIM TO RAFT.

THROW A 4, 5 OR 6 BEFORE MOVING TO 10

RAFT

**THE RULES**

**1** Each player puts a coin on a ship (two or more players can choose the same ship, if they like).

**2** Take turns to throw the die and move the number of spaces thrown. If you land on an anchor, carry out the instructions at the end of the chain.

**3** Once on land, choose any path to get you to the treasure. When you've reached it (with an exact throw of the die) make your way back to the ship. First back on board ship wins the game!

CHASED BY SNAKE! TAKE ANOTHER TURN.

FALL INTO RIVER. SCRAMBLE OUT AT 13

FALL OFF LOG BRIDGE. MOVE TO 13

STOP TO ADMIRE STRANGE BIRD. MISS A TURN.

BROKEN OARS. GO BACK TO SHIP.

PARROT FINDS SHORTCUT TO 15

CHASED BY WILD PIG. TAKE ANOTHER TURN. (QUICKLY!)

ATTACKED BY LOCALS! RACE TO 13

# MAKE A PIRATE SHIP

You will need:
a cereal box,
tape,
old newspapers,
wallpaper paste,
thin dowel,
poster paints,
polyurethane
varnish, white
paper, and
thread

Pirate ships came in all shapes and sizes— quite a lot of them were stolen from their victims! Pirates liked the swift little merchant ships best of all. These were perfect for fast hit-and-run attacks.

CUT OFF FLAPS

**1** Cut the flaps off the box and cut it in half lengthwise. Keep any spare cardboard.

**2** Cut the front and back of the box at a sloping angle, as shown above.

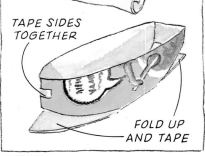

TAPE SIDES TOGETHER

FOLD UP AND TAPE

**3** Curl up the two bottom flaps, and tape in place—you'll need to cut the front flap into a point to fit.

PRESS DOWN TO MAKE SIDES SPREAD OUT SLIGHTLY

DECK

**4** Turn the boat upside down on the spare cardboard. Then draw around the shape, cut it out, and tape it inside the boat.

TAPE DECK INSIDE BOAT

**5** Mix the paste and tear the newspaper into small strips. Cover the boat with three layers (see page 11).

**6** When dry, cut the "gunwales" for the cannons (make these by rolling up some small pieces of paper and holding them in place with tape).

GUNWALE

GUNWALE

CANNON

MASTS

GLUE CANNONS INSIDE GUNWALES

BOWSPRIT

**7** Cut a small "X" on each end of the deck. Ask an adult to cut the dowel into masts. Push these through the Xs and glue in place.

**8** Glue another piece of dowel to the prow (the front of the ship) to make the bowsprit.

**9** Paint your ship and finish it with a coat of varnish. Cut sails from paper or cotton fabric, and tie them to the masts with the thread.
    Either cut pirate figures from cardboard, or use toy pirates.

# INTO BATTLE!

Pirates would lie in wait for any likely-looking ship that sailed by. Then, with flags fluttering and cannons blasting, they swept up alongside their terrified victims and scrambled aboard....

The pirates let out loud, blood-curdling cries as they leaped on deck. They also waved around a lot of pistols, pikes, cutlasses, and daggers. However, all-out battles were quite rare. Not many sailors were brave enough to fight back!

Although some pirates made a fortune from looting treasure galleons, others attacked merchant ships carrying cloth, brandy, and spices. Sometimes, if there was disease on board the pirate ship, a medicine chest could be the greatest catch of all.

Pirates often fooled their victims by flying a "friendly" flag until they were close enough to attack them. Then, to the huge dismay of the unlucky sailors, they would hoist the Jolly Roger!

# The Jolly Roger

Many pirates flew a black flag with a spooky-looking skull and crossbone design. This was called the Jolly Roger, or Black Jack. Most pirate captains had their own flag, each with a slightly different pattern. Sometimes, they also hoisted a red flag. This meant that no mercy would be shown in battle.

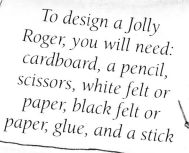

To design a Jolly Roger, you will need: cardboard, a pencil, scissors, white felt or paper, black felt or paper, glue, and a stick

**1** Sketch a design for your own Jolly Roger on the cardboard.

**2** Cut out your design. Draw around it onto white felt or paper, and cut out.

**3** Cut a square of black paper or felt and glue on the shapes. Glue a stick to the side.

# YO HO HO! (AND A BUCKET OF DOUGH)

Yet another long evening at sea with nothing to do? Try making some salt-dough decorations for your cabin...

You will need:
1 cup flour,
1/2 cup salt,
1/2 cup water,
poster paints,
polyurethane varnish,
foil, and a knife

**1** Sift the flour into a bowl. Add the salt and water, and mix well until it makes a smooth dough.

**2** Make models as shown below. Then bake at 350°F for around 30 minutes. Set them aside to cool.

**3** Paint, and when dry, give it a coat of varnish.

## DOOR PLATE

ROLL OUT THE DOUGH UNTIL IT'S ABOUT 1/2-INCH THICK

CUT A DOOR PLATE SHAPE, AND MAKE A HOLE AT EACH END FOR THE NAILS.

BAKE, AND PAINT WHEN COOL.

BEN'S CABIN

## PIRATE ON A RAFT

ROLL BALLS AND "SAUSAGES" FROM DOUGH TO MAKE PIRATE'S HEAD, BODY, ARMS, AND LEGS.

PRESS FIVE "SAUSAGES" TOGETHER SIDE BY SIDE TO MAKE A RAFT.

PRESS DOUGH THROUGH A GARLIC PRESS TO MAKE HAIR!

MOLD CHEST, BARREL, AND ANY OTHER PIECES FROM DOUGH.

ASSEMBLE PIECES AND BAKE.

# MAKE A TREASURE CHEST

Right. You've become a highly successful pirate and now need somewhere to stash all your ill-gotten gains. It's time to make a treasure chest...

You will need: a cardboard box, glue, tape, paints, some split peas, polyurethane varnish, and cardboard

**1** Cut the sides of the box, as shown in the picture.

**2** Bend the back over. Try to make a smooth curve, *not* a sharp crease.

**3** Cut the front bar, lock, and bands from cardboard. Attach to the chest.

FRONT BAR    LOCK

TAPE TO FRONT

GLUE ON SPLIT PEAS FOR "RIVETS"

**4** Cut four slits in the front. Cut two tabs from cardboard, and fold as shown. Push the tabs through the slits and tape inside.

TAB

TAB

Paint and varnish the finished chest.

## PIECES OF EIGHT

These were Spanish dollars (each dollar was worth eight "reals"). Cut some from cardboard— paint them silver, or cover in aluminum foil.

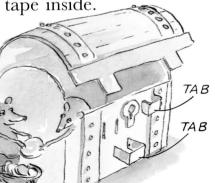

Many pirates met a bloody death in battle or were hung for their crimes. Others ended up as knights!

## Henry Morgan

No privateer ever led such a charmed life as Henry Morgan! His daring raids against the Spanish thrilled Charles II of England, who made him Deputy-Governor of Jamaica in 1674.

## Captain Kidd

Kidd was hired to catch pirates for the government but ended up a pirate himself. He was hung in 1701—people have been searching for his treasure ever since.

## Bartholomew Roberts

This interesting pirate captured no fewer than 400 ships. He was very religious, drank only tea, and liked his crew to be in bed by 8:00 P.M. sharp! Roberts was shot in battle in 1722.

HALL OF FAME

MORGAN

KIDD

ROBERTS

## Blackbeard

This alarming pirate liked to go into battle with burning fuses tied to his hair. Feared as much by his crew as he was by his enemies, Blackbeard was finally killed in 1718 by a young naval officer.

## Anne Bonny and Mary Read

These tigresses of the high seas were the fiercest fighters on "Calico Jack" Rackham's pirate ship. Unlike their captain, they were pardoned in 1720 and narrowly escaped the hangman's noose.

## Francis Drake

Francis Drake was a famous English sea explorer and a popular hero in the 1500s. His reward for privateering was a knighthood from Queen Elizabeth I.

*All but one of these pirates met their fate or made their fortune in and around the Spanish Main.*

BONNY

RACKHAM

READ

DRAKE

BLACKBEARD

Why not throw a pirate party? Planning and making things is half the fun, especially if you ask a few shipmates to lend a hand...

## PARROTS

Trace the parrot from page 32 onto cardboard. Paint brightly and cut out. Hang up with thread.

### SKULL AND

## INVITATIONS

Make an eyepatch for each guest (see page 9) and send it to them along with the invitation.

YOU ARE INVITED
TO A
**SKULL AND
CROSSBONES
PARTY**
DATE ___ OCTOBER 15th
PLACE ___ SKULL ISLAND
(TOM'S HOUSE)
TIME ___ 3 P.M.
DRESS AS A PIRATE!
R.S.V.P. or else!

## USING MUSIC

Use music and other noises to help you set the mood. You should be able to borrow a tape of sailor's sea chanties or sound effects of sailing ships from a library.

## PALM TREES

Draw some bark segments and leaves on cardboard. Paint, cut out, and tape together at the back to make palm trees.

# CROSSBONES PARTY

## PLACE CARDS

*You will need: thin cardboard, tracing paper, paints, and scissors*

POLLY

**1** Cut out rectangles from cardboard—two for each guest. Draw lines across the middles.

**2** Trace the shape from page 32 onto half the rectangles. Then cut out with scissors, as shown.

**3** Fold all the other rectangles in half. Then glue an island shape to the front of each rectangle.

# Fun and Games

Here are some good games and activities for keeping your pirate guests out of trouble...

## PIRATE PICTURES

*You will need: a roll of lining paper, scissors, a pencil, paints, and brushes*

**1** Cut several sheets of lining paper. Make each one a little bit longer than your own height.

**2** As each guest arrives, pin one sheet to the wall and ask them to strike a piratical pose. Draw around them with a pencil.

## FISHING

*You will need: two rods or pencils, thread, two magnets, paper clips, a bucket, some cardboard, tape, and glue*

**1** Tie lengths of thread to the rods and tie on the magnets. Cut 20 fish, 15 pieces of eight, and 5 treasure chests from cardboard.

**2** Tape a paper clip to each shape. Put a score on each one (say, 5 for a fish, 10 for each of the pieces of eight, and 25 for a chest).

## BLACK SPOT

*Give each player two circles cut from black paper and get them all to stand in line. Then shout GO!*

**1** Each pirate puts a spot down and stands on it with one foot. He or she then puts the next spot down and stands on it with the other foot.

## TREASURE ISLAND

*You will need: a sheet of Styrofoam, paper, some paints, and toothpicks*

**1** Paint an island on the paper and tape it to the Styrofoam. Put an "X" under the paper. Cut a paper flag for each pirate guest, and glue to a toothpick.

**3** The guests then use paint to turn their outlines into fierce pirates!

PUT DOWN LOTS OF NEWSPAPER!

Make a hat for each pirate (see page 10) and ask them to paint on their own design.

**3** Put all the shapes in the bucket and divide the pirates into two teams.

25
25

**4** A pirate from each team fishes until they get a catch. Then the others take turns.

**5** When the bucket is empty, count up the score. Award the winners a bag of chocolate coins!

**2** The pirate then lifts his or her foot off the first spot, picks the spot up, puts it in front, and steps on it!

**3** See who can reach the finish line first—anyone who puts their foot on the ground and not on a spot is disqualified!

**2** Ask each pirate to stick their flag on the island. Then check whose flag is nearest the "X"!

HANNAH
ALEX
LEILA
GEORGE

# Grog and Victuals (Drink and Food)

Luckily for your guests, the food at your party will taste about a million times better than anything the real pirates ever ate! Follow the ideas and recipes shown below.

## LEMONADE

(to protect against scurvy)

*You will need:*
6 lemons
1/2 cup sugar
3/4 cup water

**1** Grate the lemon rind. Put it in a heatproof pitcher, along with the sugar.

**2** Boil the water and pour it into the pitcher. Stir until the sugar dissolves.

## NECKLACES

Cut thread into 14-inch lengths. Use a darning needle to thread on chunks of cheese, apple, pineapple, grapes, pretzels, raisins, etc.

## CANNONBALLS

(for pirates with a sweet tooth)

## TREASURE CHESTS

*You will need:*
a chocolate mini-roll for each guest
colorful small candy (such as jelly beans or M&Ms)

Cut each mini-roll in half. Put a few pieces of candy inside and replace the top!

## HARD TACK

Buy some chocolate chip cookies—pretend the chips are weevils!

**3** Squeeze the lemons and strain them into the pitcher.
Serve chilled.

# PIRATE BOATS

Just split some rolls in half, butter them, and top with some of your favorite spreads.

Use paper and some toothpicks to make sails and masts!

For about 20 cannonballs, you will need:
1/4 pound soft cheese,
1/4 cup chopped walnuts,
1/2 cup confectioners' sugar,
1/8 cup cocoa powder,
chocolate milk powder

**1** Stir the cheese, nuts, cocoa, and sugar together until well mixed.

**2** Roll the mixture into small balls, each the size of a walnut. Roll each ball in chocolate milk powder and put in tiny paper cases.

# TROPICAL BOATS

For 24 boats, you need:
6 large oranges
2 packs of gelatin

**1** Cut each orange in half.

**2** Scoop out all the flesh. Then make the gelatin. Follow the directions on the pack, but use a little less water.

**3** Pour the gelatin into the orange halves, and put in the refrigerator. When set, cut each one in half.

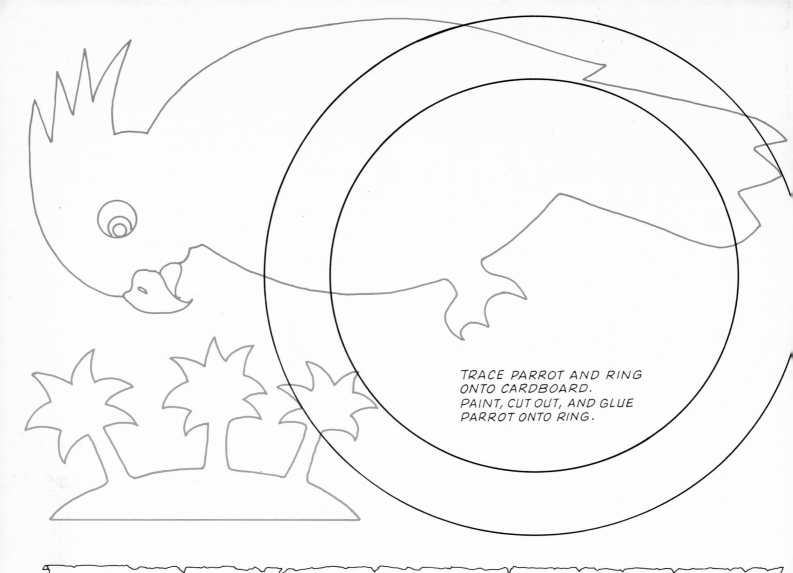

TRACE PARROT AND RING
ONTO CARDBOARD.
PAINT, CUT OUT, AND GLUE
PARROT ONTO RING.

# *Battleships*

To play this game, you'll need some paper, pencils, and another pirate. First draw a grid like the one here. Number the squares 1-13 along the top, and write the letters A-M down the side.

**1** Pirate 1 secretly marks 20 ships on his map, while pirate 2 marks 20 ships on hers.

**2** Pirate 1 calls out a grid reference—say B2. If pirate 2 has a ship on this square she must cross this off. Pirate 2 then calls out a grid reference. If she "hits" a ship on pirate 1's map, he crosses it off.

**3** The first pirate to sink all of the enemy's ships wins the game!